MW01088772

BKPM Pocket Guide for Project Managers

© 2015 by Think Systems, Inc.

BKPM Pocket Guide for Project Managers

Contents

Intentionally Left Blank

How to Use This Guide

If you are the greatest project manager of modern times, simply throw this guide in the trash; otherwise, put it next to your keyboard, in a convenient pocket, stain it with coffee rings or condensation from a cold drink, but keep it handy. This is your get out of jail free card; however, it isn't magic. It's a tool and you'll need to learn *how* and *when* to use it.

The single most difficult thing for you to learn is when you should reach for this guide. Believe it or not, you already know. You just don't know that you know and you need to become more attuned with your feelings. That's right, you're human, you have a powerful brain and a big part of your brain gives you your feelings. These are the single most valuable indicator that you need to do something different. Consider this, while managing a project, if you feel anything other than absolute control, it's time to figure out why. Feelings like anxiety, fear, concern, or perhaps worst of all, indifference, are BIG indicators and tell you that you need to be doing something other than what you are.

When you feel anything other than control, ask yourself, *"Why?"* You may know and simply need to slow down enough to realize it. Even more likely, especially at first, you'll ask yourself why and reach the conclusion, *"I have no clue."* As soon as that happens, grab this guide!

There are many useful tips in this guide including BKPM principles, Think's Rapid Control Process, project Kick-Off job aids and much more.

Using BKPM Principles for New Options for Action

BKPM principles and techniques are designed to help you make the right decisions while managing a project. You can have the best process in the world, but you also need to be sensitive to project conditions and you need to make the right decisions in order to execute.

BKPM principles and techniques provide an alternate point of view from which you can evaluate your current state. Adopting this new point of view can unlock new options for action. Not all principles apply to every situation, so the challenge is in finding the right principle for your current situation; remember there may be several.

Examples:

- You have a new project and you're trying to get your arms around it, but it just seems too amorphous and has too many unknowns. Chunking might help, so might Enumeration without Fear.
- You've identified a risk but don't have a perfect way to mitigate it. At best you have a pretty good idea how to react if it does happen. Better consider developing an Access Portal.
- No one agrees how to get going and everyone keeps suggesting more analysis to attempt to identify a solution. Don't get frustrated. Forward Motion is the principle you are look for and you may need to implement Momentum over Analysis.

BKPM Principles and Techniques

Of all of the principles in this guide, the concept of managing project as if the BKPM is sitting at a three-sided table is one of the most fundamental. Almost everything else is designed to maintain this relationship between project owners and fulfillment teams.

No project manager, not even the most highly skilled, can do it alone. Executive leadership sets the tone and provides the support; project sponsors establish the goals; the solutions team partners to do the work; and the project manager runs the

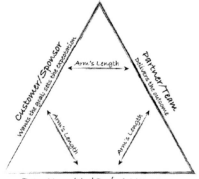

Bare-Knuckled Project Manager
Architect and manager of the plan and process

plan and process. Establishing clear goals, roles, and expectations for the different project players is a necessary precondition for the BKPM.

The following table provides a list of established BKPM principles and techniques, but it doesn't need to stop here. If you find something that works well for you, add your own to this list and use it to become a better BKPM.

 BKPM Pocket Guide for Project Managers

BKPM Principle	Description
Access (Escape) Portals	A strategy the BKPM builds into the plan to allow bridging the gap with the customer when conflict and problems arise. Access portals include agreeing about areas of relative flexibility, agreeing about responses to foreseeable risks, agreeing about approaches to unforeseeable risks and issues, and agreeing about processes for conflict resolution.
Anti-fragile	This principle applies to many things but very often to project plans and risk mitigation strategies. It is a process by which you intentionally expose your intensions to outside stressors in order to see if they hold up under new pressure or scrutiny. Whenever you have plans that are solid and buttoned up, then make them Anti-fragile.
Change Management	A process by which changes are negotiated or accepted as fact, are documented, and are rolled into outcome modification, project planning, and risk management.

8

BKPM Principle	Description
Chunking	If any process step is too large to accurately track progress, individual responsibility, external variables that may impact it, or variables that it may introduce to other process steps, it must be broken down. Chunking is the process by which a BKPM continually breaks-down project components into actionable pieces, even if the action is to break it down further.
Conflict Resolution	A thoughtful process in which you first identify your goals in order establish a strategy for resolving the conflict. A BKPM doesn't have to fight every battle, but is unafraid and will move forward with purpose if a battle is warranted.
Co-opt Risk	What happens when the three-sided table breaks down and the project manager becomes aligned with one of the remaining two sides.
Enumerate without Fear	Create a punch list. Free yourself from worrying about priority, order, or importance and simply list everything that you can think of that needs to be dealt with. Any item, large or small, can be added to a punch list. Once the punch list is established, every item can be broken down and planned.

BKPM Principle	Description
Executive Options	Risk mitigation and project control that exceeds the general ability of a BKPM. These options empower executives to work within the triple constraint model to enable large investment/authority changes that provide BKPM with new options. Executive Options generally result in Access Portals once properly Snaked.
Forced Clarification	The process by which the BKPM ensures that the customer or sponsor defines the outcome, a necessary precondition to moving forward with the project.
Forced Conflict	A purposeful situation where the BKPM sets up a direct conflict to force a resolution to an imminent process incompatibility or risk.
Forward Motion	A BKPM is committed to moving forward constantly, even when goals aren't clear (which is most of time).

BKPM Principle	Description
Guard Rails	This describes what we do to set up and pattern of execution that is pre-programmed. Example: The control phase of the RCP sets a weekly meeting and Agenda and commits to it through the course of a project. That series of committed executions, and others like it, we call Guard Rails.
G-R-E-A-T	An acronym for team building, which works best when people are clear about goals, roles, expectations, attitudes and aptitudes, and time.
Iterative Approach	When the outcome isn't clear up front, the project may go through cycles and multiple prototypes to gain increasing clarity and understanding. May be part of an agile process.
Land Mines	Land minds are numerous individual actions put in place to force forward momentum or keep action within a particular vector. Usually, land minds result in a negative outcome if hit and, therefore provide negative reinforcement.

 BKPM Pocket Guide for Project Managers

BKPM Principle	Description
Mistake Management	A process that provides a framework and directives for dealing with mistakes before they spiral out of control. It must be addressed without fear of confrontation, but also with the understanding that mistakes are rarely intentional. Look for root causes and build checks and balances to minimize the likelihood of additional mistakes.
Momentum over Analysis	A strategy used to make the project move forward regardless of unknowns. If mired down in analysis, build small achievable steps to force forward progress.
Pre-Mortem	During plan review and snaking, ask task owners to conduct a pre-mortem that creatively projects absolute worst-case scenarios. Examples: hit by a bus, down with the flu, disaster power outage, test environment equipment failure, business fails regulatory check, etc.
Recovering Value	The BKPM alternative to ineffective "lessons learned," a strategy to extract value from the project experience and results to benefit the organization and future projects.

BKPM Principle	Description
Risk Management	A six-step approach to managing recognized risks that results in contingency planning and/or communication (access portal development).
Shredders	These are barriers to project success. Unlike normal barriers that can be overcome at the PM level, shredders are cultural barriers in your organization that may only be overcome by applying constant pressure at the corporate level.
Simplicity	The best approach to any activity is simple, direct, and effective. Elaborate planning introduces variables and risks that cannot be tracked and managed without expending a lot of energy.
SMART+ER	An acronym for a set of standards used to validate and measure project outcomes. (Specific, Measurable, Agreed to, Realistic, Time-constrained, plus Ethical and Rewarded.

BKPM Principle	Description
Snaking	The process of weaving back through everyone who has a role in plan tasking to make sure they have had a chance to provide a risk evaluation, personal commitment to deliverables and dates, and general awareness of task dependencies. (Attributed to a Chevron CPDEP concept)
Spectrum Analysis	A thought process step in which you challenge your instinctive perception of a risk, constraint, or possible solution. Slow down and think best case, worst case and what could possibly go wrong to invalidate your assumptions of the situation.
Strategic Marketing	Just getting things done isn't always enough. Sometimes a PM must strategically market or communicate plans and accomplishments in order to maintain momentum and drop barriers to implementation of planned activities.

BKPM Principle	Description
Tempo	"I think fast, talk fast, and I need you to act fast..." -- Winston Wolfe. We use tempo as one technique to establish control in a project, whether intentional or not. Thinking fast and moving fast for a client makes it easier for them to contribute and they appreciate the sense of urgency
Three-Sided Table	A BKPM approach to project management in which the BKPM owns the process (but not the outcome), the sponsor or customer owns the outcome (but not the process), and the partners and team own the technical solution.
Triple Constraint	The traditional set of constraints that shapes the world of any project, consisting of the time constraint, the cost (or resources) constraint, and the mandatory performance criteria, ranked in order of flexibility and driver, middle constraint and weak constraint.
Unafraid of Conflict and Confrontation	A core competency of a BKPM that results in proactive responses to unknown, risk resolution and planning, and communication.

Personality Traits of a BKPM

BKPMs have a set of personality traits that describe them at their very core. The ideal BKPM, the BKPM Archetype, is highly operationally disciplined, focused on the project management process and the team, only slightly concerned with maintaining personal relationships, and not very concerned with getting into the creative aspects of developing options for technical solutions.

This chart represents the natural resting state of an ideal Bare Knuckled Project Manager. The darker area in the center is their natural resting state; however, everyone can expand their zone in time of heightened awareness. A tactical BKPM's zone expands to be even larger, but similar.

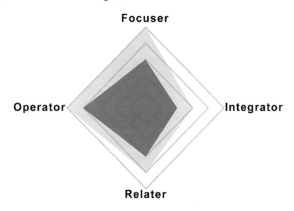

Direct

# Focuser	# Operator
Positive Traits	**Positive Traits**
• Determined	• Detailed
• Controlled	• Accurate
• Commanding	• Organized
• Authoritative	• Methodical
Negative Traits	**Negative Traits**
• Domineering	• Obsessive
• Autocratic	• Rigid
• Hard-Headed	• Compulsive
• Tyrannical	• Slow
# Integrator	# Relater
Positive Traits	**Positive Traits**
• Imaginative	• Listener
• Creative	• Team Player
• Energetic	• Loyal
• Future-Directed	• Sympathetic
Negative Traits	**Negative Traits**
• Unrealistic	• Unassertive
• Manic	• Conforming
• Unable to Finish	• Gushing
• Poor Time Management	• Indecisive

Task ... *People*

Indirect

Operating Within the BKPM Zone
Not everyone's natural preferences and personality traits match the BKPM Archetype. When projects are running well and you are not experiencing stress, most PMs can force themselves to operate in the BKPM zone.

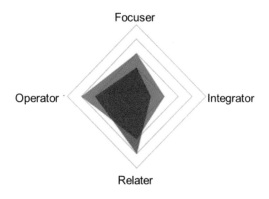

If your natural resting state zone differs from the archetype, you will need to **recognize** when you're operating outside of the zone and **expend energy** to get back into it. Use **BKPM Principles** to get control.

Think's Rapid Control Process

1. Discovery & Immersion

Organize and consume all historical project knowledge and artifacts. Includes meetings with key individuals, review of documentation, etc.

Deliverables: working knowledge of the project.

Participants: Think Account Manager, Strategic PM, Tactical PM, Client Stakeholders

Duration: Usually 8-24 hours, depending on complexity of the project.

2. Planning

Multi-pass planning starting with "Straw Man Plan" development, reflection of plan with key individuals, resource development, timeline/outcome balancing.

Deliverables: Draft Project Charter, Project Plan, Resource Plan, List of Risks, other supporting documents as needed.

Participants: Strategic PM, Tactical PM, Client Stakeholders

Duration: Typically 24-80 hours, depending on complexity of the project.

3. Validation & Risk Mitigation

The Draft Plan is subjected to the stress of validation and risk mitigation to determine fragility. Involves tough discussions of how risks will be confronted as they emerge in the project.

> **Deliverables:** Near-final Project Plan, Resource Plan, Risk Plan, Schedule, Approval to Proceed, and agenda for the Kick-off Meeting.
>
> **Participants:** Strategic PM, Tactical PM, Client Stakeholders
>
> **Duration:** Typically 8-40 hours, depending on complexity of the project.

4. Kick Off

Think presents the final project documentation package (all documents created in previous steps) to the stakeholder team. Ownership of steps is cemented and ground rules for engagement are discussed and accepted by team members. Final adjustments are made and advertised.

> **Deliverable:** FULL PROJECT CONTROL.
>
> **Participants:** Strategic PM, Tactical PM, Client Stakeholders
>
> **Duration:** Preparation requires a few hours to a day of work (2-8 hours) culminating with the Kick-off meeting.

5. Active Management & Control

Once the kickoff is complete, the Tactical PM will actively control the project by socializing it with appropriate personnel, managing the tempo, conducting weekly review meetings, and by providing reporting and tracking updates. Risks encountered are confronted aggressively.

Deliverables: Project Tempo, Weekly Reporting, Active Risk Management of the Project. The process is now owned by the Tactical PM; the outcome of the project is fully owned by the project sponsor.

Participants: Strategic PM (as needed for meetings and risk mitigation), Tactical PM, Client Stakeholders

Duration: Varies depending on the level of complexity of the project, from 8-40 hours per week by the Tactical PM and a few hours per week by the Strategic PM, as determined by the resource plan.

Kickoff Readiness Review Process (Immersion)

The Kickoff Readiness Review (Immersion) Process is a subset of Think's Rapid Control Process designed to qualify the project scope, deliverables (high level chunks), identify risks and mitigation plans, and agree on commitment dates with the Customer/Sponsor. This process allows the Project Managers to present what was identified in the Discovery and Immersion step and correct any (discrepancies) in the early stages of planning without exhausting any of the triple constraints.

RCP Kickoff Meeting

During Think's Rapid Control Process Kickoff Meeting the SPM and TPM should accomplish seven key objectives to be ready to present and review with the Customer/Sponsor.

1. To Do List
2. Project Kickoff Commitment Dates
3. Project Plan High Level Chunks (Deliverables)
4. Define a Rough Scope Statement
5. Define Key Resources
6. Define a Risk Registry
7. Define Open Action Items

Each of these specific areas define a starting path to get Rapid Control. These can be defined with the Think team in a short working session, ideally in a 'war room' environment using a white board or large 'Post It' pads. This allows for a collaborative session and creating a starting point for which the TPM can start planning. Each of the objectives are described more in depth below.

To Do List

The 'To Do List' should be a quick action list of items to review/kick off in the RCP Kickoff Meeting. These initial items should include the following;

1. Review Notes (SPM/TPM)
2. Project Plan (TPM)
   a. Create STRAWMAN Plan
   b. Upload Plan to Think Corporate SharePoint Drive
   c. Add High Level Chunks (Deliverables) to Project Plan
3. Project Charter (SPM)
   a. Use Notes to Define Scope Statement
   b. Draft Initial Draft
4. Risk List (TPM)
   a. Add initial mitigation statements
   b. Add to Project Summary Report
5. Resource List
   a. Add to Project Plan
6. Budget Review (SPM with Customer/Sponsor)
7. Next Steps
   a. Create Project Summary Report (Draft)
   b. Create Executive Summary Report (Draft)
8. Commitment Dates
   a. Draft Plan Commitment Date
   b. Hardened Plan Commitment Date
   c. Kickoff Readiness Review Meeting Date (Customer/Sponsor Meeting prior to Kickoff Meeting)
   d. Kickoff Project Commitment Date

This list can include additional items but is used to keep the team moving through the Kickoff Readiness Review process. It is critical to discuss the Commitment Dates and ensure these are attainable and realistic dates as these are the earliest indicators to the Customer/Sponsor of Think's performance.

Commitment Dates

As previously stated, the Commitment Dates are the first promise to the Customer/Sponsor and need to be dates that will not move. The four dates allow for the Tactical Project Manager to get immersed, meet with key resources and adequately understand the scope of work, resources needed and the time the project will needed given the Driver and weak constraint.

Draft Plan (STRAWMAN) Commitment Date:

This is the date the Tactical Project Manager agrees to have a rough project plan in place and is ready to review with the Strategic Project Manager. It is likely that the plan will still have unknowns as this date approaches, but it is important that the TPM's plan aligns with the SPM's vision. During the Draft Plan Review meeting the SPM will walk through the project plan with the TPM to ensure the direction of the project is on target and discuss changes/edits and next steps. Additionally any new risks can be discussed for a mitigation plan.

Hardened Plan (anti-fragile) Commitment Date:

This is the date the Tactical Project Manager agrees to have a hardened project plan ready for review with the Strategic Project Manager, prior to the Kickoff Readiness Review meeting with the Customer/Sponsor. This date is typically set a couple of days prior to the Kickoff Readiness Review meeting

24

so the plan should be as close to complete as it can. The TPM should be prepared to complete a 'dry run' walk-through as if presenting to the Customer/Sponsor and be prepared to make any last minute updates prior to the Customer/Sponsor meeting.

Kickoff Readiness Review Meeting:
This is the date both the Strategic and Tactical Project Managers agree to have a project charter, project plan, a risk registry with mitigation plan, resource allocation report and project summary report ready for presenting to the Customer/Sponsor. This meeting is where the Customer/Sponsor has the ability to ask questions about the plan, therefore it is critical to gain confidence that the project plan is thorough and has enough risk assessment to avoid missing the project completion date.

Kickoff Project Date:
This is the date the Project Managers and the Customer/ Sponsor agree to kick off the project and begin executing against the project plan.

Project Plans

It doesn't matter what tools you use to manage your project plans. What matters is that they contain the level of detail needed to maintain control of the project process (usually task, duration, work, start, finish, precedent, and resources needed), are easily updateable, and communicate realistic tasks and durations.

General Rules (can always be bent for a good reason):

1. **Tasking should be tracked in chunks** no greater than 5 days, but preferably no greater than every 2 days, either as task complete or percent complete. A great deal of effort must go into maintaining project status. Really, task duration depends on how resources are linked to it. If a single person is responsible for a task that lasts two weeks and that's all they are working on, and it cannot be chunked further to measure progress, then it can be allowed, but caution should be used.

2. **The project plan must remain achievable**. You must not allow tasks to go un-completed without documenting them and adjusting the plan to accommodate (either through re-planning or use of slack). You must have a manageable way to keep them under control; usually, this involves properly vetting and snaking with all parties. Minor interruptions might be OK, but they may snowball, or worse, develop as blind spots in your planning.

3. **Schedule risk mitigation**, sometimes called contingency, should be allocated to those tasks deemed riskiest. It should not be considered a slush fund that can be consumed by any task that is running long. There is no way to accurately predict down-stream impact otherwise and poorly applied contingency is a sign of a project plan that is not well thought out.

4. **"Everyone, review this," is not a reliable strategy** for communicating task expectations or for learning of potential issues. The PM is likely to be the only individual that can consume all of the detail in a good project plan. If you want good feedback and team awareness, then tasking may need to be broken-out per individual. You should ask (snaking principle):
   a. Can you get this finished as planned?
   b. Do you know of anything you need in order to accomplish this and can I help you get it?
   c. What is the worst thing that could happen that would prevent you from finishing (apply pre-mortem principle)?

5. **Visibility is required** to make your plans anti-fragile. Print them and post them frequently (weekly at least). Require that team members and stakeholders review them. Include a pdf version with every project report. The more visibility a plan has, the better accountability experienced in projects. If everyone knows what is expected by them, their role, deadlines, and deliverables, they are more prone to own them and report possible expected slippages.

Weekly Status Report Template

Project Name			Status as of:	mm/dd/yy
Begin:	mm/dd/yy	Executive Sponsor:		
Projected Completion:	mm/dd/yy	Project Sponsor:		
Active Phase:	Select...	Project Manager:		

Executive Update	Overall Health:
Monthly high-level accomplishments and major activity forecast	

Team Update (Health)

	Weekly update used to provide status to sponsors, stakeholders, and team members.
?	

Major Milestone Updates

?	Milestone 1 {MM/DD to MM/DD}	
?	Milestone 2 {MM/DD to MM/DD}	
?	Milestone 3 {MM/DD to MM/DD}	

Current Risk Items

ID	Risk/Impact Description	Mitigation Action	Back-up Plan	Owner	Impact / Risk	
					?	?
					?	?
					?	?

Current Action Items

ID	Date	Description	Actions Taken	Owner	Status
	mm/dd				?
	mm/dd				?

Out of Scope / Parking Lot

ID	Date	Description
	mm/dd	

Change Control Register

ID	Classification	Description	Request/Approval	
	?		Requested by:	mm/dd/yy
			Approved by:	mm/dd/yy

A Weekly Status Report (WSR) is a critical tool for project managers. There are hundreds of "correct" formats for WSRs. The key to a WSR is that it communicates what is important and that it is easy and accurate to maintain. It doesn't matter if the report is maintained in Word, Excel or in a central database. What matters is that they are effective for the project.

Many WSR templates are pushed down to PMs from a PMO and are rarely focused solely on enabling a project manager to control their projects; they typically place additional burden on PMs so the PMO can report information that is important to the PMO. PMs should test WSR templates to make sure they are simple, direct and effective, and that they do not cause undue burden on running the project effectively.

Here are a list of fields that we often find are needed in a WSR:

Field	Description
Project Name	Easily recognizable name
Status as of	Date (mm/dd/yy)
Begin	Project inception date (mm/dd/yy)
Projected Completion	Date (mm/dd/yy)
Active Phase	Discovery & Immersion, Planning, Validation & Risk Mitigation, Kick Off, Active Mgmt & Cntrl, Close Out

Executive Sponsor	Executive (e.g., CFO) name
Project Sponsor	Technical (e.g., CTO/CSO) name
Project Manager	Strategic PM / Tactical PM name(s)
Executive Update	Monthly high-level accomplishments and major activity forecast Profit/Loss statement; cost projection Schedule tracking and projection
Overall Health	Color-based health indicator – green, yellow, red, hold (red diagonal lines)
Team Update	Color-based health indicator + Weekly update used to provide status to sponsors, stakeholders, and team members
Major Milestone Updates* (repeat as needed)	Color-based health indicator + Milestone Name + Date range (MM/DD to MM/DD) + Status description

Current Risk Items*	Quick reference ID + Risk/Impact Description + Mitigation Action + Back-up Plan + Owner + Color-based impact rating (L, M, H) + Color-based risk rating (L, M, H) +
Current Action Items*	Quick reference ID + Created date + Description + Actions Taken Log + Owner + Status (New, In Prog, Closed)
Out of Scope / Parking Lot	Quick reference ID + Created date + Description
Change Control Register	Quick reference ID + Classification (budget, time, features, risk) Description and impact on project Requested by + date (mm/dd/yy) Approved by + date (mm/dd/yy)

* Completed items get moved to archive one cycle after being reported as complete

Made in the USA
Charleston, SC
14 May 2015